Now I Sit Me Down
to Write My Memoirs

Now I Sit Me Down to Write My Memoirs

Marian C. Pilcher

To order additional copies of this book, contact:
Xlibris Corporation
1-888-795-4274
www.Xlibris.com
Orders@Xlibris.com
46205

Contents

Introduction 11

Chapter 1   In the Beginning 13
Sub stories   Haans MacGregor................................15
               The Country Doctor (short story)...........16

Chapter 2   Back to me 19
Sub stories   Back to the farm................................20
               The Boarding House 21
               The Rat and I (short story)..................21

Chapter 3   School Days 23
Sub stories   High School Days 24
               The Cost of Things............................25

Chapter 4   My Work History................................26
Sub stories   At Home in the 50's............................27
               About the Area..................................29
               More Work Experience 29
               More of Ozalid 33

Chapter 5   My Husband.....................................37
Sub stories   One Train Ride (short story)................37

Chapter 6   Bits and Pieces 40
Sub stories   Aside 40
               My Dogs 40

Chapter 7   Let's Go West 42
Sub stories   The Dave Pratt House (short story) 43

Chapter 8   The Christopher Family..48
Sub stories   Pioneer Courage (short story) 48

Chapter 9   Later—The Move East 53
Sub stories   Odds and Ends..54

Chapter 10   My Most Significant Experience 56

The manuscript of My Memoirs is dedicated to my father, Dr. William Christopher, who didn't live to see me graduate from High School, much less to appreciate the stories I wrote about him. He was a pioneer in medicine, an unassuming practitioner, and a good friend to many. He was father, hero, teacher and friend. I love you, Dad.

William Britton Christopher
1860-1933
May his memory be eternal.

It is also dedicated to William and Jenny Bennett, the couple who took me into their hearts and gave me the love and nurturing I needed to become a person strong enough to face the hardships of life. They are sadly missed, even to this day.

The stories and incidents in My Memoirs are true, based on the stories my father told to me or as told to him by his father, or lived as experience. The names are factual to protect the innocent.

Introduction

My purpose in writing My Memoirs is to make my reader chuckle, perhaps shed a tear or two and surely learn something about our American history.

My readers may be skeptical of my remarks and memoirs. They ARE in my memory—not told to me.

I have a sixth sense, sometimes referred to as ESP. Even today at 89, more than half of the time, I can tell who is on the telephone before lifting the receiver or checking the caller ID.

Read on, Friend, with an open mind.

—Marian Pilcher

Chapter 1

In the Beginning

Dr. William Britton Christopher and Agnes Ophelia (Birdsall) Christopher ushered me into the world in the house at 402 South Liberty Avenue, Union, New York. Dad was 58 and Mother was 42. Being born of older parents, for all intents and purposes, I could have been mongoloid. But I'm perfectly normal—apparently. Although when I say I remember being born, it might raise an eyebrow.

It was dark where I was—dark, warm and wet. This dark, warm, wet thing stroked down my face. Cooler air struck me. The overhead light was cloudy and blurred. It hurt my eyes. I slid out into a pair of strong hands. He's hanging me upside down?! And whapping my backsides?! "Ouch!" What's that noise? A squeak? A baby crying? Warm hands rubbed me all over with oil. Nice! And a warm blanket to cover me! That's nice. Strong arms encircled me. "Ummm nice."

The house was a three family, brick structure my Father designed and built mostly himself. He wanted a special roof but the helper didn't understand. So Dad made a mock-up from cigar boxes. Then the man knew exactly how to proceed. The walls were double-bricked, making wide window sills, good for plants and for me to hide behind the curtains when we played hide-and-seek when I was a toddler. The trim and floors of the house were real walnut. Dad laid the floors himself in pattern. All the rooms were spacious and airy—truly a beautiful home. The sun room door was usually kept closed because the wrap-around windows caused the room to be unusually warm, especially in summer. There was a dumb waiter in the kitchen on the first floor to take something to the cellar without carrying it by hand or bring something up to the first floor. All my life, I had hopes of owning this home, but it never happened. Finances and circumstances interfered.

The house afforded many memories for me:—the extra lot Dad used as his garden. (Oh, those vegetables, berries, and asparagus were really delicious!) My escapades—I played in the third floor apartment when it was vacant One day, I leaned too far out over the porch railing and fell onto a pile of dirt. I didn't hurt anywhere so I just went back into the house.—the time Laura and I got our feet tangled going down the front steps—She fell on top of me and went back into the house crying. I went on to school, had a headache about all day and still have a three-cornered dent in my forehead from the corner of the concrete steps.

Dad was born in Galena, Illinois, in 1860, Mother in Willow Point, New York, in 1876. They were married Christmas day, December 25, 1900.

The way they met was interesting. Agnes hadn't been feeling well, so she went to see Dr. Will. His examination made him believe she was suffering from waste poisoning. He asked her if she evacuated regularly. She said "Yes." So he looked for some other cause. But the more he examined her, the more he was sure his original diagnosis was correct. Then he asked her, "How regularly?"

Her reply was "Once a week."

Dr. Will stifled a chuckle but a look into Agnes' pretty face hooked him for life. He asked if he could see her again on a less professional basis and the die was cast

When Dad brought his bride home, his five year old nephew fell in love with her.

"Can I buy her?" Lee asked.

"Well, I don't know. How much are you prepared to pay for her?", Dad asked.

Lee fished a nickel out of his pocket and handed it to Dad who put the nickel in his pocket

A few days later, when Lee came into the house, Mother was sifting on Dad's lap. Lee was disgusted. With both hands on his hips, he exclaimed: "Well! I didn' buy her for that pupose!"

Mother broke her engagement to a young lawyer—who later became Major of Binghamton, N.Y.—to marry Dad. They had five children, the first, Carol, was born December 24, 1901. She passed away in 1941 of pneumonia. The second, Frances Birdsall, was born April 27, 1903. She passed away at age 97 of stomach cancer. The third, William, was born August 16, 1904. He later said, "Life is unfair. Everyone else in the family has a brother but me."

As a young teenager when he was playing with friends, when darkness approached, Mother stepped out onto to the porch and called, "Willlieeeee, Willieeee".

He hated that name and wouldn't answer or go home until later. I often wondered if Mother's call was so offensive, why he didn't just go home when it began to get dark. You see teenage rebellion is not a new thing.

Bill passed away in 1967 of lung cancer. He was a smoker and couldn't give them up until he was told he had cancer. Too late, then.

The fourth child was Laura Lillian born January 16, 1916. She was a big baby, weighing over 10 pounds. Mother had a friend who had a three month-old and when the babies were laid side by side, newborn Laura was bigger than the three month-old baby. Laura passed away in 2003 at age 87 of complications of Diabetes.

The last of the litter was me, Marian Elizabeth, born April 24, 1918. Mother had originally named me Thelma Juanita. Dad's brother, Ernest's wife, Eva, was hard to get along with and at the time of my birth she and Mother were on the outs. When Aunt Eva came over to see the new baby and remarked that Thelma Juanita was a pretty name, Mother immediately changed it to Marian Elizabeth.

Uncle Ernest was also a doctor—of diseases of women. Evidently the term gynecologist hadn't been invented yet. One day one of Uncle Ernest's patients gave him a sample of urine in a shampoo bottle. Uncle Ernest was in a hurry to make another house call, so he set the bottle on a small table just inside the front door. When Aunt Eva saw it, she remarked she wondered how Ernest knew she needed shampoo. She immediately washed her hair and wondered why the shampoo didn't foam the way it should have. Because none of the family was overly fond of Aunt Eva, we had many a chuckle over her "shampoo".

*   *   *

Haans MacGregor

Dad took whatever the patient could afford to pay for his services—produce, eggs, chickens—what-have-you. One patient gave him a race horse named Haans MacGregor. The horse had a will of its own and one day when Dad had to go out on a call, the horse acted up. Dad grabbed the horse by its head, using leverage taught him in Syracuse Medical University, threw him to the ground, sat on him and whipped his rump. When Dad let Haans MacGregor up, from that day forward, he knew who was the master.

One day as Dad entered the barn, he saw the water faucet running full strength. He questioned his son and nephews, accusing them of leaving the water running. Every one of the boys declared his innocence. But how else could the water be left running? Dad found out. He went to the barn one day and caught Haans MacGregor turning the faucet to get a drink. Now the trick would be to teach the horse to turn the water back off.

One of Dad's patients asked Dad why he let Mother go out alone with Haans MacGregor. Dad's reply was, "Why not, she's a better horsewoman than I am."

Being a well-trained race horse, Haans MacGregor wouldn't let another horse pass him on the road. Dad said he never lost a race with the stork as long as he had him. In the 1920's. the stork brought babies and dropped them down the chimney. The Dr. had to get there in time to catch the baby—or so I was told. The procedure is different now, I understand. After Haans MacGregor died, Dad bought the first Model T Ford ever owned in the town of Union.

The Model T served him well, putting on many miles as he took care of his patients. During the flu epidemic of World War I, my brother, Bill, then a teenager, drove the car between patients' homes while Dad snoozed in the back seat. When Dad visited the patient, Bill slept in the car. That way, Dad was able to tend to his patients 24 hours a day. He lost only one patient during this time. The woman was getting better, but Dad specifically instructed her to stay in bed and rest a few more days. She thought as long as she was better, she could get up and get supper for the family. The husband called Dad and told him his wife was having a relapse. Dad said, "No, she isn't having a relapse, she's already had one."

Dad traded the old Model T for a 'newer model' in 1932, mostly due to my brother's insistence. Unfortunately, because Dad had an artificial leg, he couldn't manage the modern car and had to hire a driver. My brother drove him around for a while and then I got my driver's license early so I could do it.

++++

When I worked for the Army in a medical supply depot, I wrote for the Caduceus Courier, the house organ. One of the stories I wrote was *The Country Doctor*.

++++

The Country Doctor

We have all known a country doctor, smiled at his wry humor, made faces as we swallowed his bitter medicine or perhaps wondered what kept his life from becoming humdrum. Let me tell you of a country doctor it was my privilege to know.

He treated all who came to him and practiced the theory that all persons were honest and if his patient didn't pay him, it was because they couldn't right now but would later. Dr. Will treated Ministers free because his father was a Minister.

When we knew him, practicing in a small town, treating his patients in a kind, sympathetic manner, telling stories of his life as a boy in the West with never a boastful word of his accomplishments, it was easy to forget he was a successful surgeon not many years ago and won recognition from the New York Medical Association for performing the first operation of its kind.

But his wife would gladly brag of her husband's accomplishments and awards.

Dr. Will would rather tell you incidents like the time when Model T's came into being and he went to try one out. At that time, a driver's license wasn't required to operate a car. The salesman took the prospective buyer around the block and pointed out the throttle, spark, and the brake, along with instruction for properly cranking the car. Then, the buyer drove home.

As Dr. Will came back to the barn with his brand new car and started to drive it under the shelter, he said quietly but firmly, "Whoa". As the car refused to obey, pulling back on the steering wheel, he said a little louder and firmer, "WHOA—WHOA!!—WHOOOA". As the car went through the back of the barn, Dr. Will remarked to no one in particular. "This thing has gone too far!"

Dr. Will was a great man, a successful doctor who never lost the common touch, yet if you should ask him to what he attributed his success, his only answer would be a twinkle in his blue eyes. A second question, *"What did education do for you?"* brought forth the answer, "Well, without education, I would have been an everyday fool."

In the morning, the towns people discussed Dr. Will's bringing twins into the world breech birth to a woman who could speak no English; with no one assisting, washing and oiling the babies himself. The husband spoke and understood enough English so he was able to relay the Dr's messages to his wife. i.e. "push". "relax" etc.

That evening, they discussed his sudden death and the fact that he left his books so that the unpaid bills would never be collected, and knew that a truly great man had left their midst.

++++

To my knowledge, in his practice, Dad was the first to use the "sugar pill" on his diabetic patients. Word spread of his success and one patient, Verna Roberts, came up from Starrucca, PA., a 40 mile trip. Her foster son, Sanford Furman, brought her. Usually they furnished the chicken for our dinner and stayed to fellowship afterward. Later, Dad took a tumor off Sanford's temple. Dad let me help him with that operation, but he squelched my hopes of becoming a doctor. Medical school was too hard for a woman, he said. Back then, when the father said "No", that settled the matter for good. No pouting, no whining. But it was the biggest disappointment of my life.

Verna and Sanford became good friends of the family. Later Sanford married my sister, Laura. After Verna and Dad passed away, Sanford came up to call on Laura. I thought he intended only to continue the friendship between the two families but when she told me they were going to get married, I thought 'that will be a fiery marriage.' Laura was an 'old maid', set in her ways, and Sanford was a 'confirmed bachelor'. Surprisingly, though, I have never met a more compatible pair.

After Laura had her baby, Sanford spent one night with us. We had a Seth Thomas clock that chimed every 15 minutes as well as on the hour. In the morning, Sanford looked as if he hadn't slept well. He said, "That clock sure chimes a lot at midnight." It did—28 times.

We had gone to the hospital together to wait for the baby. I was in the room with Laura when I noticed she was uncomfortable. I checked and then went out to the nurses' station to ask someone to check her. The nurse gave me such a knowing smile and said,

"Oh, we'll have quite a wait yet"

I said, "The baby's hair is black."

It took her several seconds to realize what I had said, then she flew into Laura's room and whisked her into delivery.

*   *   *

Chapter 2

Back to me

When I was 10 months old, Dad became very ill. With the breadwinner laid up, and no income coming in, Mother went to work in the Endicott Johnson shoe factory, the primary employer of that time. This left my older sister, Frances, who was 16 at the time, to care for the family. This particular day, the furnace went out and the house was frigid.

Friends of the family, William and Jenny Bennett, dropped by. I was shy and hid behind Frances' chair. She rocked back over my foot. It was so cold it didn't bleed even though a large three-cornered piece of flesh was torn from my arch. Mrs. Bennett suggested they take me home with them until the situation at home worked itself out.

I cried, of course. When they arrived at their farm in Maine, N.Y., Mr. Bennett struck a match with his thumb nail and lit a lamp fastened to the wall. The Christopher house had electric lights and I remember thinking that was a strange way to get light but that was the way it must be on a farm. Our meal was bread and milk—a farmer's supper. Tears were still streaming down my checks and into my mouth. I wondered why the bread and milk tasted so salty.

After I got used to the farm and the Bennetts, whenever I went back to the Christopher house, I got homesick to go back to the Bennett's. I did visit my biological parents from time to time, but I spent most of my life with the Bennetts. I called Mr. Bennett Daddy and eventually called Mrs. Bennett Mother.

After one of the visits to my biological parents, when I was 14 months old, Dad Christopher brought me back in a buggy. Daddy Bennett met him, also in a buggy, at the intersection in the town of Maine. Dad's buggy was headed one way. Daddy Bennett's the other. I was transferred into Daddy Bennett's buggy and the two men talked a few minutes. Finally, Daddy Bennett said, "Will, why don't you give her to me."

I held my breath in anticipation. That arrangement would suit me fine. Dad replied, "You can have her."

Daddy said, "No, I mean really give her to me."

Dad replied, "You can have her."

How's that for a gift of a child?

Why would I prefer the Bennetts over my parents?—the difference in the home life of the two families. In the Christopher household, I was the 'fifth calf'. I felt like an outsider and was treated that way—no outward expression of affection between my parents—or from any member of the family toward me. Cold! So many times when I expressed my opinion or likes or dislikes, I was told, "You're not the only pebble on the beach."

Only on two occasions, have I recollection of my mother holding me—when she nursed me and the morning she was making pancakes for the family. She was holding my sister, Laura, and me on her lap. We were both fussy. Hot grease on the griddle exploded and hit me on my leg.

But in the Bennett household, a loving atmosphere prevailed between William and Jenny—loving, not mushy. Both were generous with their kisses on my cheeks—tousling my hair—encouraging me, whether it was my accomplishments or in conversation. My comical remarks brought a chuckle. In the Bennett household, I was made to feel important, wanted and loved, as against the Christopher household where I felt I should be unseen as well as unheard—as if I was a 'mistake' and they blamed me for it.

Back to the farm

My sister, Frances, married when I was three. She brought her husband to the farm to introduce him to the Bennetts. I disliked the man immediately. After they left, I 'wrote' her a letter telling her what a mistake she had made, that I thought Ralph was a scoundrel. The ensuing years proved me right. I gave my scribbled letter to Mother Bennett to read and she handed it back and said, "Read it to me." So I did.

Another incident of my 'foresight' that might raise an eyebrow—in 1975, my daughter-in-law's Mother passed away. My son and his wife lived near Chicago and planned to drive straight through to Chenango Bridge, New York. I asked the Lord to wake me every hour on the hour so I could pray them safely here. He did. Every hour, I sent up a prayer for their safety. This went well until three o'clock in the morning. I prayed for them but felt no peace so I prayed again. Still no peace. I woke my husband and told him the kids were in trouble and asked him to pray with me. We had our prayer session, taking turns praying until I felt peace in my heart. When my son called the next morning, I asked him how the trip went. He answered, "It got pretty rough around three o'clock this morning. I didn't think we were going to make it."

++++

The Boarding House

Daddy Bennett died when I was six. Mother Christopher came to the Bennett house and asked Aunt Jenny if she wanted her to take me 'home'. I'll never forget her answer—it's no wonder I loved her.

She said, "I've just lost my husband and now you want to take my daughter away too?"

Aunt Jenny kept boarders. That was how she made our living. She was an excellent cook and could stir up a meal in no time flat. But she kept no recipe file. When she saw a recipe she liked, she read it and threw it away. She catalogued that recipe in her head and could recall it any time she wanted to make it. She never measured ingredients yet everything came out perfect and delicious. You should see the mess I made when I tried that procedure.

She charged the boarders $1.00 a day and packed them a lunch if they worked. Remember this was in the 1920's. One boarder, Harry Beebee, stayed with us for years. One boarder's weekly payment, $7.00, bought groceries for the rest of us, a total of three big grocery bags of food. Aunt Jenny carried two home and I carried one.

At this time, we lived next to the Union Forging Works in Endicott, N.Y. The Forging Works was a breeding ground for wharf rats and the morning I discovered one in the bathroom, I wrote *THE RAT AND I*.

The Rat and I

Perhaps life in a boarding house is always interesting or perhaps it was because I was the daughter of the boarding house keeper that I got a ring-side seat to all the fun. Mother always was an early riser and I didn't try to change her. One morning after I heard her leave her room, I heard the unmistakable thud of a falling body. I sat bolt upright in bed but when I realized the sound wasn't loud enough to be a person, I laid back down.

A few seconds later, Mother burst into my room very excited.

"Get up—quick! There's a great, big, rat in the bathroom—the biggest I have ever seen!!!

I lunged out of bed and quickly slipped into my robe. Looking around for a lethal weapon, all I could find was a yard stick broken in two almost in the center. I charged toward the bathroom armed with my trusty broken yard stick—with

Mother at my heels. Opening the door ever-so-cautiously, I thrust in my nose and one eye. There he was!! I opened the door very wide and jumped at the rat. One wide swipe with the yard stick knocked him off his perch and he scrambled out of the bathroom, through the dining room and into the kitchen.

I went after him in full pursuit but when I got to the kitchen, I didn't see him. I walked carefully into the center of the room—searching the room at eye level. Bending a little, I searched it again at waist level. One level lower, on hands and knees, I again searched carefully around the room.

"Guess I must have lost him." I said only seconds before I saw him—not more than two feet away from my face—next to the stove leg, sitting on his haunches with his tail wrapped around him, cat-fashion. I held my position and stared at him unblinkingly.

He held his position and stared right back unblinkingly. He out-stared me and every ounce of courage drained from my body.

"Get one of the boys." I called over my shoulder to my Mother, who was hovering in the doorway, holding her robe above her knees. (I said this louder than was necessary to convince the rat I wasn't afraid, but I think he knew the truth all the time.)

George came out of his room sparingly dressed, broom in hand and knocked the rat out from under the stove. The rat started toward the dining room. Mother was watching from behind me in the doorway. We both moved fast but the rat moved faster. and was almost upon us. Mother squealed and jumped into a chair. I squealed and jumped into a chair (Same chair.) The rat squealed and jumped into a chair. (Same chair.) Mother squealed and jumped onto the dining room table. I followed—so did the rat. George reached us, luckily before either of us were bitten, knocked the rat off the table and killed him.

My knees were weak as I wobbled off the table thinking how easily a broken yard stick and a lot of foolhardiness can create false courage.

On the next rat-hunting trip, COUNT ME OUT!!

*   *   *

At one time, things got a little rough financially for Aunt Jenny and she asked my Father for board money for me, he promptly brought me home to live with them. I was living with my biological parents when my Dad passed away in 1933. Eventually, I went back to live with Aunt Jenny.

Chapter 3

School Days

Laura and I were in the same grade though High School, even though we went to different schools—you might say we went together separately. She didn't start until she was seven. I started when I was four. The Bennetts and I lived three doors from Loder Avenue School. I watched the children going by and thought that was the greatest thing ever. Aunt Jenny got tired of me asking why I couldn't go too, so when I was four, she dressed me up and told me to go. I took the school steps one at a time. When one of the teachers asked my age, I promptly told her "four". She asked me when my birthday was and I told her. She told me to go back home, I was too young to start school. I started to cry. Such a disappointment! The other teacher said,

"Let her stay, she won't last the day out." But I did and stayed in school until graduation from High School in 1935—with honor.

On one of my visits to my biological parents, they lived on a farm in Brockham Town. Being country, the school had one room and one teacher for all grades. When I arrived, the teacher asked what grade I was in and my age. I told her I was five and in second grade. She didn't believe me and gave me colored toothpicks to play with.

The second day, when I was sent off to school, I decided I wasn't going to go and be humiliated with colored toothpicks again. I detoured off into a field, and sat down in the tall grass. One of the family saw me and sent my brother to take me to school. I expected to be punished, but instead he took me by the hand and walked me the rest of the way. He assured the teacher that even though I was actually five, I was in second grade and I was allowed to join my peers.

During Dad's illness, the Liberty Ave. house was traded for a farm. My unmarried brother was supposed to work it, but his dating, late home-coming and lack of desire to get up in the morning when the cows were bawling to be milked, caused Dad to lose the farm.

Not long after my experience with the one-room school, Dad fell going down the cellar steps and broke the ends of two of his ribs completely off. A few days later, I saw him standing in front of a full length mirror, performing surgery on himself to remove the ribs. He did the complete operation on himself under local anesthesia.

I watched in awe as he injected the numbing substance into his chest, incised the area, removed the loose rib ends, sutured the wound and bound his chest With an example like that, how could I not decide to be a surgeon like him!! That was the day I made up my mind.

++++

High School Days

At the time Laura and I were in High School, we lived in the Village of Maine, New York, some nine or ten miles from Union-Endicott High School, so we were dependent on the school bus for transportation. Catching the early bus pushed our schedule somewhat. If we missed it, we had to wait about an hour for the last bus.

One day, for whatever reason I don't remember, we missed the early bus and decided to spend time in our homeroom working on our homework. The janitor came and found us there alone. For some reason, it upset him and after chiding us for missing the bus, he said, "I'm going to lock you in." He did, and we immediately decided on our means of escape. By piling the desks on one another, we were able to open the high windows. I helped Laura out and then she helped me out. I was halfway out the window when the janitor decided he better unlock the door and come back. A strange expression crossed his face and I imagine he realized if we reported him, he would lose his job. Jobs were hard to come by in the 1930's. I could see no reason to climb back down that stack of desks, so I exited the window.

We didn't report him, however, and from that time on, he went out of his way to be nice to us. The situation didn't bother me that much, but to Laura, that janitor was something to be completely ignored or snubbed.

When I graduated from High School, I wanted a school ring. Mother Christopher bought Laura's without question, but when I asked her for help with mine, she said, "My God girl, do you think I'm made of money?" Aunt Jenny pawned the watch Daddy Bennett had given her so I could get my ring.

The Cost of Things

I have sewed since I was old enough to hold a needle. (At the age of 3, I designed and sewed a bonnet for my doll.) One could purchase good material for 5 to 10 cents a yard in the 1930's. Luxury material might run as high as 20 cents a yard. During the summer months, when I was in High School, I worked for the State, counting traffic by hand, for one day, twelve hours, and received $2.80. This was enough to buy material for dresses for school for an entire year.

My sister, Laura, and I looked so much alike our teachers couldn't tell us apart. They called us the Christopher twins. To confuse them further, I often made Laura a dress exactly like mine.

As a matter of fact, we three sisters looked alike—3 chips that didn't fall far from the block. One day, a man stopped me on the street and said, "Hello, Frances."

"I'm not Frances."

"Oh, Laura."

"I'm not Laura, I'm Marian."

++++

Chapter 4

My Work History

My first job was with Rhinevault Trucking Company in Endicott. My shorthand teacher recommended me and I was hired on the first interview. I started as secretary to the Office Manager and later became Office Manager. That's where I was when I met John Roy Pilcher, my first husband. Those were lean years. I was working a six-day week for $10.00. Roy's Army pay was $12.00 a month, but back then, bread cost 5 cents a loaf, gasoline 10 cents a gallon. From there, I went to work for the Army during the war.

I started out in Kendea, near Geneva, New York. The Army built a wooden building, but with no central heating system. There was one portable heater available for each floor. When we called the supply office and told them we were freezing, we got the heater for an hour or so but it was soon taken away because some other office was cold. One day we got the heater for about ten minutes, not nearly long enough to take the chill off, before it was whisked away. In a little bit, I called supply and complained of the cold. The Supply Master said, "Okay, I'll send up the Armstrong Heater."

Fine, at last we were going to get some heat. About five minutes later, after a knock on the door, in walked a young man who looked like a line backer. Our Armstrong heater!! We started to laugh but evidently he wasn't in on the joke. He looked puzzled until we explained. He didn't stay however.

Every few days. there would be a notice on the bulletin board, "It has come to the attention of the Commanding Officer that . . . whatever the problem was." One day, the notice read, "It has come to the attention of the Commanding Officer that too many things are coming to the attention of the Commanding Officer".

Since it was a military installation, anything military was top priority, anything civilian could wait. A cereal salesman from General Mills called several days in a row to speak to the Supply Officer for a chance to bid on the cereal concessions for the Cafeteria. Each time when asked "Whose calling, please?", he answered "Jack Dunn". Time after time the answer was, "The Captain is away from his desk at the moment" . . . or "The Captain is in a staff meeting and can't be disturbed." . . . or "The Captain is out in the field and isn't expected back until Wednesday." A light began to dawn. The next time he called and was asked "Who's calling, please?" be answered "General Mills" and was put right through.

At Home in the 50's

On September 10, 1950, we got our joyful bundle so I became a stay-at-home mom for 14 months. We never hid the fact that the boy was adopted. We didn't discuss it at every meal, naturally, but if the subject came up, we talked about it as if it were the natural, wonderful occasion that it was to us. When Verne started school, and one of the children chided him about being adopted, he replied, "That's all right. Your mother HAD to keep you, but my mother CHOSE me."

When it was deemed necessary for Roy's salary to be supplemented, I took a job with the Chenango Bridge Telephone Company as night operator. Then, our headset consisted of overgrown ear muffs and a speaker that looked like an inverted cow horn.

Only party lines were available at this time, up to eight families on one line. The telephone numbers were determined by a combination of long and short rings, and rang into all phones on the line.

With so many people using actually the same phone, common courtesy dictated limited personal use and immediate release if an emergency arose. Such was not always the case—as when my barn caught fire.

I was in the barn taking care of my kennel when I noticed the blaze. I ran to the house only to find two women talking on the phone.

"Please let me have the line—my barn is burning"

A few seconds of silence, but before I could reach the crank. the conversation continued.

First woman: "Did you see Ella Drury at Olson's auction?"

Both laugh.

Second woman: "Yes, I saw her. She looks like a baby hippo in that purple outfit."

"Please let me have—"

First woman: "Someone should tell her how awful she looks."

"Please—let—me—have—the—line!"

Second woman: "Why don't you tell her?"

"Please—oh, pleeease . . . ." I'm in tears, thinking, "Alice, you are a witch—spelled with a B. I've got to get my dogs out."

Alice: "Well, I guess someone wants the line."

June: "Guess so. You going to Grange Tuesday?"

"Please—let—me—have—the—line. My—barn—is—on—fire."

Alice: "Plan to. I'll pick you up—usual time."

"Please, oh, please . . ."

June: "Call me soon. Bye."

Alice: "Bye."

Grabbing the crank, I called the operator to get the fire department and gave them directions.

I ran back to the barn to empty the kennel. My foster boys were getting the dogs out of their cages. Danny was so excited, he just put the dogs over the fence instead of putting them in their play area. Two dogs ran away. One froze that night and the other was never heard from.

By the time the volunteer firemen arrived, the barn was too far gone, but they did save the house.

On the switchboard, one evening during a severe electrical storm, lightening came in on my headset. That was the beginning of my hearing loss. One night—a farmer's telephone was out of order but when he jiggled the receiver on his phone, I heard the rattle and plugged in. He had a sick cow and wanted to call the vet. He wanted to be sure he could reach me if necessary, so I left my listening key open all night for him.

Late one evening—a Druggist in Binghamton called, frantically wanting a certain family's number. Unfortunately, they had no phone.

"Can you call a neighbor?" he asked.

"Sorry, we can't give out nearbys." I replied.

All excited, he told me a young man had come in for a prescription for his sick baby at the same time an elderly man came in for a prescription for his heart medicine. They had talked a few minutes at the counter when the young man inadvertently picked up the elderly man's medicine and left. Fortunately, the elderly man checked his prescription right there.

The frantic Druggist was about to tear his hair out for fear the father would give the baby the wrong medicine. What could I do???? How could I get help??? There was no one on the switchboard with me that I could send to the young parents home. Aah, the County Coordinator, the forerunner of our 911 system. After I explained the problem, he sent a deputy to the young man's house and fortunately got there in time. When I called the Druggist back with the good news, he offered to send me something—"anything—just name it" for what I did. I told him, No, I couldn't accept anything but if he was so inclined, he could send up a box of candy for the entire crew. He did. The next morning, a five pound box of his finest chocolates arrived by special messenger, but by the time I came on duty, only two pieces were left.

Every year, the workers at my husband's place of employment went on strike. Usually, it lasted only a week or so. When I was working, the strike didn't affect us a great deal. But one year, while I was still a stay-at-home mom, the strike lingered on for six weeks. My husband had picket duty one day a week. He was paid $2.89. That was our grocery money for the week.

I bought thee pounds of macaroni, a pound of oleo, a large can of tomatoes, a half pound of cheese and a can of evaporated milk. The $2.89 covered it. Day one, I made plain macaroni soup, the next day, macaroni and tomatoes, the next, macaroni and cheese, and then started the round again. We survived, but to this day, I can't look a stick of elbow macaroni in the face.

++++

About the Area

Years ago, Binghamton had a W.T. Grant store, about two steps above a five-and-dime. I did a lot of shopping there. One day, I was in the back of the store and as I looked up, I saw a woman looking at me. I thought, "She looks familiar and she looks as if she recognizes me. I wonder why she didn't wave." I went toward the front, looking for the woman, but she had disappeared. As I turned to go to the rear to finish my shopping, I bumped into the minor-covered pillar that held up the ceiling. No wonder the woman looked familiar, I had seen my own reflection!!.

Grant also had a restaurant that offered good food at a reasonable price. I went there for lunch one day. They had a horse shoe shaped seating area. The waitress took the order and delivered it from the center of the horse shoe. After she brought my food, I bowed my head to give thanks. She appeared almost immediately and asked if the food was all right

"Oh, yes, it's fine" I assured her. Before she turned back to the kitchen, she said, "I saw you smelling of it so I thought there must be something wrong with it."

More Work Experience

At one time, I worked for Jacuzzi Brothers in Binghamton, New York, makers of pumps from 1/3 horse power you could hold in your hand to pumps big enough to produce the hydraulics that ran an elevator for one of the tallest buildings in Los Angeles.

My desk sat snug up against the partition between the office and the warehouse. On the other side of the partition, a shelf held the percolator. I could feel the vibrations of the coffee making. When they stopped, I called to the Sales Manager,

"Mr. Glock, the coffee is ready."

He knew I hadn't left my desk or opened the warehouse door so he asked me how I could tell. "I heard the light go on." I told him.

Mr. Glock weighed every week on the platform scales in the warehouse. After one weighing, he lamented a big weight gain of ten pounds. What had he eaten last week that had caused it? What could he do differently this week to take it off? The weight gain mysteriously disappeared the next time he weighed and he never found out that the big, bad, weight gain was my foot on the back of the scales.

Stuart, our warehouseman was an excellent and willing worker. So much so that he was promoted to Office Manager after the former Office Manager was let go. It was my job to reconcile the petty cash fund each week. There began to be a shortage I couldn't account for. Thinking I was negligent somehow, I made up the shortage. At first it was a dollar or two, but every week the shortage got larger until it amounted to ten dollars. That was too much for me to make up out of my small salary, so I told Stuart about it. He admitted "borrowing" a few dollars now and then. I was slightly miffed and informed him if he borrowed any more, to put a chit in the box so I would know where the money went. That should have forewarned me for the trouble later but it didn't. I'm a trusting soul. Stuart offered to work Saturdays nearly every week. He handled the entire transaction of any sales. When I attempted to reconcile the serial numbers of the pumps that were sold with the invoices on which they were billed, every week, there were several that I couldn't account for. After an exhaustive search, I took the books to Stuart. Each time, within a very few minutes, he 'found' the illusive information. It wasn't until I asked a customer to pay for a pump he had purchased, that I was informed he had paid for it at the time of purchase. Stuart bad handled the sale on Saturday.

Realizing there was some thievery going on, the number two warehouseman and I called the main office. This brought the Sales Manager who talked with Stuart. The Sales Manager then informed me that Stuart had confessed and was very contrite. His conscience bothered him so he was glad to get it out in the open.

"Can you still work with him?" the Sales Manager asked.

I asked him if the reason Stuart confessed was perhaps due to the fact that we had reported him. He didn't seem to know that and as a result, let Stuart go. I hated to have to do it, but otherwise I might have been suspect.

I met Stuart sometime later and of all things, he was mad at ME because he had lost his job.

One day on my way to work, I came to a hole in the road, down to the reinforcement mesh. In New York State, that meant a depth of at least 12 inches. I went down into the hole very carefully, and carefully eased out and went on my way.

In our town, there was a very conscientious motorcycle patrolman named Moss. It was rumored he gave his Grandmother a ticket for going one mile over the limit On this particular day, going my merry way, I heard the tinkle of a motorcycle and looked in my rear view mirror. Moss!

A glance at the speedometer told me I was going 30 miles an hour in a 15 mile an hour zone. What could I do? I knew he was after me, so I immediately pulled over.

As he came alongside, I started searching for my driver's license. I couldn't find it. What I did find was a back seat driver's license I had picked up as a souvenir on one of my travels. Back then, we had paper licenses and the back seat driver's license was also paper and the same color as my regular license. For want of something to do, I handed it to Moss.

The back seat driver's license was issued by G.M.I. Nervous and gave me the right to misdirect, pester and otherwise annoy the driver of any vehicle. Moss read it with a slight smile as I continued to search for my license.

"Do you use this?" Moss asked me.

"All the time" I told him. By this time I had found my license and handed it to him. He handed it back and said, "Next time be more observant." I'm sure I'm the only person living or dead that Patrolman Moss didn't give a ticket.

We received a letter from a man in the Finger Lakes region who wanted to put water from the lake into his cottage. He gave the offset, lift, and other requirements. I worked the equations and wrote him the recommended pump and accessories he needed to do the job. I signed just my name—no Mrs.

In a few days, he called and asked for Marian Pilcher.

"Speaking." I answered.

He gasped. "You're a woman!"

"Yes," I replied, "that's what I understand."

"Well! I don't want to talk to no woman. Don't you have a man there I can talk to?" he asked angrily.

"Yes," I replied. "Hold on for a couple of minutes. I'll get Ron the warehouseman for you."

I explained the situation to Ron and told him what unit I had recommended. "But if you think some other one would be better, feel free to change it."

Ron considered the specs and settled on my recommendations. The customer bought the equipment. A man's recommendation would work, but a woman's? Never!

Because of my knowledge of pumps, the head of G.L.F. gave me a glowing recommendation and offered me a job in their warehouse, when Jacuzzi Bros. moved their operation to New York City.

I told Gicondo Jacuzzi it was not a wise move, but they moved anyway. In Binghamton, the haulers called us every morning to see if we had freight for them that day. My phone conversation went like this for several minutes:

"Jacuzzi Bros . . . yes we do."

"Jacuzzi Bros . . . no, not today."

"Jacuzzi Bros . . . yes we do."

In New York City, the haulers serviced their regular customers before picking up Jacuzzi freight. Shipments sat on the loading dock for days waiting pick up. They lost a lot of customers because of that. I never did get to tell Gicondo "I told you so."

It was fun working for them. They treated me like a queen. But all good things must come to an end.

My last job in industry was for Ozalid in Vestal, New York. I worked there long enough to be within reach of tenure when I was laid off. It gave me the determination I needed to start my own business—preparing income tax returns. I've done it ever since, 41 years now. For 26 of those years, I instructed the AARP Taxaid program counselors, and served as counselor 26 years as well.

Last year, my volunteer work for Taxaid was as a Greeter, screening the people as they came in. I could determine if the people didn't need to file, or if they needed additional papers. One of the greatest thrills was being able to help those patrons who were deaf with my being able to 'speak' sign language. I took 5 semesters of sign language so my Granddaughter could communicate with me. She can hear but doesn't speak. Not to be able to express my thoughts would be a virtual prison for me and I hoped we could communicate as she was taught some sign language in school.

Back Seat Driver's License

Issued To
Marian C. Pilcher

Who is hereby granted the right to misdirect pester and otherwise annoy the driver of any vehicle.
—G.M.I. Nervous

More of Ozalid

My husband worked for Ansco, originally named Agfa Ansco. The Company was owned by Germany and ran by two German brothers, Heinz and Adolph. Heinz was neatness personified, Adolph wasn't and chewed tobacco. After Heinz watched Adolph spit a string of tobacco juice in the general direction of the spittoon and missing 99 percent of the time, he slid open the glass partition between the two offices and said, "Adolph, better should yer spit der winder out den da floor on!"

When suspicions had been confirmed that the main purpose of Agfa Ansco was not film making but to spy on the United Sates, the Government confiscated the company and changed the name to Ansco

A Government worker (I hesitate to call him a mole) discovered wireless messages were being sent from the brother's offices at Agfa Ansco to German Headquarters. One series of messages gave explicit directions for a German submarine to navigate our waterways to enter New York Harbor.

The Medical Depot has moved upstate from New York City along with more than half of its employees. After a phone call from a relative in New York City to one of our employees, the news spread throughout the Depot. The Commanding Officer was informed there was a German U-boat in New York Harbor. He immediately called us to general assembly and told us "It is just a rumor, pure unadulterated rumor. Don't be alarmed. There is NO WAY a German U-boat could penetrate our coastal waters."

No doubt this statement was for morale purposes because I have a photograph of that U-boat IN New York Harbor. It was taken by a sailor on Harbor duty on that day in 1943. I doubt many Americans realized just how close our homeland came to being attacked.

I would rather have been told the truth—"yes, a German U-boat had reached New York harbor, but the crew has been captured and the submarine confiscated." An undisclosed number of German prisoners were housed at the base in Muskogee and—according to my husband—were treated better than the soldiers. Whether that was where the U-boat crew ended up, I couldn't say. Actually, it seemed to me there were more prisoners in that building than would be necessary to man a submarine.

After my husband had been sent to Oklahoma, I received a letter in a strange handwriting, informing me he had been wounded on maneuvers. The Company was ordered to crawl over a live mine field. The point man tripped the mine. Shrapnel penetrated his jugular vein and he bled to death on the spot

My husband was next in line and shrapnel hit him in the arm and side so he was hospitalized. As soon as I could arrange leave, I went to see him. By this time, he was ambulatory and we played quoits. I got a ringer. The prisoners in the barracks next to the hospital sent up a cheer. That whole barracks was used for the prisoners.

In 1947, we took a trip to New York. The German U-boat was a tourist attraction. For a fee, you could go down into its interior. Not me, I'm claustrophobic.

++++

After Jacuzzi Bros, I worked for the Engineering Department of Ozalid, the sister company of Ansco. It was fascinating to watch an idea progress from someone's mind—to paper—to a mock-up—to the finished product, a reproductive machine using the diazo method—Ozalid spelled backward.

My boss was Robert Goodman, a small man about 5 feet 3 inches tall, weighing about 110 pounds soaking wet. He answered the phone himself because he said it would waste my time since the call would be for him. He always left the door open between our two offices and I never paid any attention to his conversations until one day after he answered the phone, he said

"Just a minute." and closed his office door. Then my ears picked up to try to hear what was said. If I had had a glass, I would have put it to the wall between us.

When he was off the phone, he came into my office and sat down. He asked if I knew what that was all about

"No idea" I replied. He told me the Personnel Manager had informed him the Company was trying the 'bump' system that unions use. The girl who was promoted when I was hired to take her place, would be coming back and I would be sent somewhere else or fired. Mr. Goodman asked the Personnel Manager

"Is that an order?"

The Personnel Manager replied, "No, but that's what we would like you to do."

Mr. Goodman told him, "I've finally found a good girl and I want to keep her."

That saved my job. The Personnel Manager was 6'4" and weighed approximately 280 pounds as against Mr. Goodman's 5'3" and 110 pounds. After that, to me Mr. Goodman was ten feet tall.

The Company did Mr. Goodman a dirty, forcing him to retire early, and got a recruit from New York. The one who took his place was as different as day is from night. Mr. Feitzinger was over six feet tall, big boned, not fat, just big. However, he had absolutely no knowledge of the job or what was expected of him. I had to train him.

He wasn't the first boss I had to train but I didn't let it bother me. Resentment rots only the container it is kept in. That's the way it was back then—a strong bias against women holding anything but subservient positions. Gender over qualifications every time.

When Mr. Feitzinger was learning, he was considerate and sweet as sugar but as soon as he felt he knew his way around, he soured, finding fault with everything I did or didn't do. One of my jobs was to go to the mailroom at 8:00, pick up the mail for 20 Engineers and Draftsmen, circulate it, pick up their outgoing mail and take it back to the mailroom. Mr. Feitzinger chided me because I wasn't sitting at my desk at 8:00 each morning. I never did master the art of being in two places at once.

The Feitzingers had a mischievous toddler who locked his Mother out when she hung up clothes. She had to go to a neighbor's house, call her husband to come home to open the door. It tickled me to have to relate the message time after time that the boy had locked his mother out. I felt a man as smart as Mr. Feitzinger thought he was, should come up with the idea of putting a key outside for her use. Or suggest to his wife that she put the toddler on a leash and take him out with her. Of course, I wasn't about to suggest that to him. I'm sure the rest of the Engineers knew what had happened when I interrupted his coffee break, whispered in his ear and he left, suddenly. I confess I smiled a little at his embarrassment after he left.

Joel Bravo, one of the Draftsmen and I were kindred spirits in levity. Joel's job was to make a mock-up of the machine coming off the production line. After he had it painted in whatever color was selected for it, it was hard to tell his mock-up from the real thing. Joel swirled the last vestige of spray paint on a piece of plywood about 10" by 12". The result looked very much like the work of the famous monkey artist. He brought it to my office and presented it to me as if it were a Rembrandt. I accepted it as such and hung it on the wall opposite my desk.

The Plant Manager, who was into surrealist paintings, came down one day and that painting caught his eye. He stared at it face-on for several seconds, then bent his head first one way and then the other staring intently at the painting. He then twisted his body so he was practically standing on his head and stared at it some more. With a mutter of "It doesn't do anything for me" he went on into Mr. Feitzinger's office

Mr. Goodman and I had a good working relationship. If heard a rumor, I told him and if he heard one, he told me. When I heard a rumor of a coming layoff after Mr. Feitzinger came, I told him. I came out of his office with my head under my arm. It turned out the rumor was true and I was caught in it. I didn't think I would be because I was the only girl in the Department to do typing for the 20 Engineers and Draftsmen.

That fateful morning, one of the Engineers, who had worked there 15 years, went into Mr. Feitzinger's office and came out looking sick. He was recently married with two babies in diapers. I thought, 'Yes, there's one.' Then one of the Draftsmen came in and left—he was mad! I thought 'Yep, there's two.'

My lunch hour was from 11:30 to 12:00. Mr. Feitzinger came out of his office at 11:20 and sat across from my desk. He told me I was going to get caught in the layoff.

Surprised, I asked, "I am?"

He said, "Yes, Hilda, the Plant Manager's secretary, will be down after lunch. You can give her fifteen minutes instruction and then you can go any time."

I have never cowed before any boss in my work history, so I said, "Mr. Feitzinger, I was on this job a whole year before I felt comfortable, knowing what I was doing. I doubt Hilda will catch on in 15 minutes."

But then I said, "Oh, well, the Lord will take care of everything."

He was so sure I would break down and cry! He couldn't have looked more surprised if I had slapped him in the face with a dead fish. He was speechless for a few seconds, then said, "Ummm, ummm. I wish the Engineers and Draftsmen felt like that."

All of the Engineers and Draftsmen relied on my memory where certain items were bought or what Company sold what they were looking for. When Mr. Feitzinger was in my office with the bad news, one of the Engineers stuck his head in the door and asked me the purchase order number for something. I told him from memory, but it didn't phase Mr. Feitzinger a bit

When HilIda came down, I told her I had written a procedures manual. "Some things you do every day, some things once a week, some things once a month and some once a year. Here is the manual. Have fun." And I left.

To go home from Ozalid, I used an access road ending at a cross-road with a traffic light. This light went from green to red, back to green and was directly opposite the light on the main road that went green, amber, red, amber and back to green.

I was waiting at the light on the access road. A man behind me could see the main road light change to amber and he tooted at me to move out. I checked the light ahead of me. Still red. No way am I going to move on a red light! I looked at him in my rear view mirror for 15 seconds, then turned around and looked at him through the back window for at least 15 seconds, then I smiled, waved and blew him a kiss which took another 15 seconds. By this time, the light ahead of me had gone from red to green and back to red several times. The look on that driver's face and his moving lips told me exactly what he thought of me and probably all women drivers in general. As soon as the light ahead of me was green, I moved out. I stopped at a nearby mall and so did they. His wife came up to me with a smile and said, "You handled that just right back there".

I expected when Ozalid laid me off, the building might crack, but I really didn't expect it to be demolished and a shopping mall to be built on the site.

+++++

Chapter 5

My Husband

Roy and I were married December 25, 1939. He enlisted in the Army a few days later. He volunteered for Hawaii because it was a two-year hitch. The war broke out and he was there until 1945. He was at Pearl Harbor on Pearl Harbor Day, guarding the munitions dump, now the National Cemetery, about a half mile from the attack. I didn't hear for almost a month whether he was alive or dead. I was counting up on the calendar when he would be home as he had 28 days left to serve, when President Roosevelt broke in on the radio program and said the Japanese had bombed Pearl Harbor and war was declared. In shock, I knew he wouldn't be home very soon.

While stationed in Hawaii, be was returned to Oklahoma to start a cadre of the famous Rainbow Division. I was able to visit him out there and from an experience I had, I wrote *ONE TRAIN RIDE*.

One Train Ride

The war years brought many things I would like to forget but also some I enjoy remembering. One of these is my trip West. My husband had been returned to the States after three years of overseas duty and was stationed in Muskogee, Oklahoma. I had planned for several weeks to visit him for our anniversary, our fourth but the first we had been able to share.

My trip to Chicago was wonderful, in an air-conditioned coach with practically all the comforts of home. But the severe winter weather and the extra burden of wartime passengers made the train late into Chicago. When I inquired about my train out and was informed it was all ready to leave on track 9, I ran full speed ahead and stepped into the train only seconds before it started to roll. I was very proud of myself—considering two collisions but no casualties in the rush.

I found a seat without any trouble—but my womanly intuition warned me something was wrong. When the trainman started calling off the stops and ended his long winded delivery with "Local to Gallion". I knew what it was. Bright child that I am, I had nearly broken my neck to catch a milk train.

Deciding to make the best of a bad situation, I removed my coat, hat and shoes and curled up in the seat to sleep. This was really an accomplishment—considering almost six feet of physical structure and a narrow antiquated train seat. No sooner was I completely asleep when I was suddenly and rudely awakened. (I vow to this day, he put his foot on my chest) while an impatient masculine voice was saying, "Look alive! Get yourself together! They are holding the Limited for you on another track. Hurry now!!"

It took me several seconds to get almost awake and with the trainman's insistent, "Hurry now, if you miss this train, you'll have to wait 24 horns in Gallion!", I slipped into my coat, threw my hat in the general direction of my head, gathered my packages in my arms and staggered sleepily after the trainman. My feet didn't track and looking over my armful of bundles, I discovered my shoes were on the wrong feet. I attempted to change them in the middle of the tracks, but the snow was too cold and the trainman too insistent.

The loose ends of my armful gave way, and a package dropped. The trainman picked it up, put it on top of my armful with a most reproachful look, still pleading, "Hurry! If you miss this train . . . ." With a not too-gentle-push on the elbow, I was on the Limited. A chuckle from the porter greeted me as he helped me find a seat.

Still too sleepy to see any humor whatsoever in the situation, I continued my nap and must have slept through the change of trains in Gallion for the next I remember, I was being awakened for Muskogee.

I stepped off the train expecting my husband to be the first bystander. Rather disappointed, I proceeded up the dimly lit walk to the station. I noticed soldiers of every size and shape lining the benches on either side of the walk and stopped to size up the sleeping men. Some were too short, others too wide but seven were excellent possibilities. Seven times, I gingerly lifted a garrison cap to peer into the sleeping face and seven times I muttered, "Oh, excuse me."

Having to think the situation over, I went into the station. I had sent my husband a wire telling him what time I would arrive and I felt the least he could do was meet me at the station. After an hour of waiting, I was very upset.

I studied the sign on the door opposite me and just before I exploded, I said angrily to the soldier on the other end of the bench, "You go in there and if there is a soldier asleep on the couch, you wake him up and send him out here. You tell him his wife is tired of waiting!" Only a few minutes passed and out came a sleepy, wrinkled soldier. Ooooops!—wrong soldier!!!

Calling Camp was my only alternative and I was informed the message would be delivered at reveille at 6:00 A.M.—more than three hours hence, and there was no way I could be absolutely sure he was there! At 10:30, my husband called back. He had just been given the message.

After I found out where reservations had been made for me and how to get there, I started walking. I had been assured before I left home that my bags would arrive the same time I did and I wasn't travel-smart enough to bring some freshening-up aids just in case.

I realized, after several quizzical glances that I looked like a chimney sweep. Oh, well, not much I could do about it, so I smiled right back as if I always went that dirty—and promised myself when I got to the hotel, I would soak for an hour in a luxurious bath.

During our trip, the trainman had come through the coaches warning a tunnel was ahead and we were to close our windows. One person decided he could wait a while before he had to close his window. Before long, we entered the tunnel. The black, thick soot from the train stack came in that open window and sprayed each of us generously, in spite of several passengers' attempt to hold the curtain tight to the window.

Upon my arrival at the hotel, the room clerk shook his head emphatically. "No marriage license—no room!" That, too, was packed in the bag that hadn't arrived. I sat down in the lobby thoroughly disgusted and very tired, musing over the happenings of the past 48 hours—amazed that so much could happen all in one train ride.

*   *   *

My husband was sent to Europe with the Rainbow Division and was on the Maganole line Christmas Day, (our anniversary). The Company came under heavy enemy fire. Roy felt a sharp jolt on his side where his flashlight hung from his belt. The bullet penetrated the front shell, the battery and dented the back shell. That flashlight saved his life.

Chapter 6

Bits and Pieces

Aside

I admit this incident is a rabbit chaser. It doesn't have much to do with anything except my life has been filled with incidents that tickled my funny bone, then or later. I still chuckle over this one.

Friends, Merium and Howard, planned a trip out of State and needed a ride to the airport. After the bags were checked, fortunately, there was a wait for the plane out because Howard dumped a juicy load in his britches.

Merium took him into the men's room to clean him up and asked me to stand at the door and divert traffic. A man approaches.

"Sir, there's an emergency in there."

"Oh."

In a few minutes, she came out with Howard's wet shirt and handed it to me. "Would you mind swinging this around to get out some of the water?"

"No, not at all . . . be glad to."

Flap . . . . spray flap . . . . spray flap. A man approaches.

"There's an emergency in there."

Every man turned away but one. Emergency or no, he was a man on a mission.

Flap . . . flap . . . flap . . .

Flap . . . flap . . . flap.

My Dogs

Not all my life was devoted to work. For years, I raised Poodles—teacup, toy, and miniature. The kennel and the barn burning were mentioned earlier.

Starting with one dog, I ended up with 14 breeders. I was President of two Kennel Clubs and stewarded in dog shows. There can be only one winner of a dog show. So when there are two dogs that deserve to be winners one is called Best in Show the other is Best of Opposite. One of my toy males won Best of Opposite. In other words, a female won, but my dog was just as good, except it was a male.

Later, the little male lost his hearing, but he could see. I had a toy female that was blind, but she could hear. When I let them out, the male walked near the female to keep her from running into anything. When they were ready to come back in, I spoke to them. The female could hear me and somehow relayed to the male that I wanted their attention. When he looked at me, I motioned for him to come in. Then he would herd the female in the right direction and up the steps into the house. The first dog in history to learn sign language, perhaps?

But enough already! Let's go West.

Chapter 7

Let's Go West

I enjoyed hearing my Father tell incidents that occurred when our Nation was young . . .

My Grandfather, Rev. Christopher, helped settle the West. He was married to Lucinda Pine, daughter of Rev. and Mrs. Pine. They had three children, Anna, William and Ernest.

Today, we would call Granddad a Church Planter. Whatever town he chose, there never was a Church, but they always had a Saloon. Granddad made friends of the Saloon Keeper so the bar would be closed for the hour Granddad preached—opened up right afterward, of course. When the congregation got big enough, they built their own Church and when the Church got strong enough to support a Preacher full time, Granddad moved to another town.

You have heard of Wild Bill Hickcock? He wasn't the renegade he was reported to be. A magazine writer embellished and even fabricated Mr. Hickcock's experiences so his magazine would sell more copies. Mr. Hickcock was a Christian, and a personal friend of my Grandfather.

One day a group of rowdies came into town, boasting they were going to break up Granddad's meeting. Granddad told Mr. Hickcock. He answered. "I'll take care of it." The people gathered for the meeting and Granddad went through several, "Well, I guess we could sing another song" and still no sign of Mr. Hickcock.

When Granddad realized he could wait no longer, he started the meeting. True to their word, the rowdies started a ruckus. Suddenly, a deep voice came from the rafters, "That will do, boys." Mr. Hickcock had been up there all the time.

Mr. Hickcock gave Granddad one of his pearl handled revolvers. It was a beautiful piece as guns go, perfectly balanced and in good working condition. Granddad gave it to my Father. I saw it not long before Dad passed away, but a few days after his funeral, it was gone. I'm convinced my brother-in-law stole it and traded it for a bottle of wine. He was an alcoholic and did the most despicable things to satisfy his thirst. Think what that gun would be worth today!!

One of the stories Dad told me was of the man who went out with his hunting dog to get some rabbits. The dog started chasing a rabbit, and the man noticed the rabbit made several circles back to a certain log. He apparently ran through the log, and the chase was renewed. Later the man discovered there were two rabbits. One ran the course for a while, then went to the log. That was the cue for the rested rabbit waiting in the other end of the log to pop out and continue the chase. And they say animals can't think!

*   *   *

Another story: After several sightings of a woman in white who motioned with both hands for men to join her in the woods, a posse was sent out to bring in this woman of ill repute. They found a very large white hare, with exceptionally long ears, a native of that time, sitting on a tall white tree trunk. She had a nervous habit of flipping first one ear and then the other. A little imagination turned an innocent hare into a lady of the evening.

Dad told me these experiences of the barber in his town. The barber had recently been converted and was enthusiastic to witness to his customers but he lacked the knowledge. The barber had the man in his chair draped with the cape. After stropping his razor, he stepped around in front of the man with a straight razor in his hand and asked, "Are you prepared to die?"

"Not today," shouted the man as he yanked off his cape and darted for the door.

One day, a famous gunman swaggered into the barbershop and demanded a shave. He said with his hand on his gun holster, "And if you cut me, I'll shoot you dead!"

Calmly, the barber replied, "I'll shave you, take a seat."

The shave went smoothly. The gunman again patted his revolver holster and said, "Mister, you just saved your life. You know, I really would have shot you if you had cut me."

"No, you wouldn't", the barber replied. "If I had cut you, I would have slit your throat before you could reach for your gun." Bravado left that gunman like air escapes from a balloon. Swoooosh.

Another of Dad's stories inspired me to write *The Dave Pratt House*.

The Dave Pratt House

David and Beryl Mason drove along the white concrete highway, enjoying the bright sunshine, the beauty of the countryside, the display of nature's handiwork reserved solely for the fall of the year—and most of all, enjoying each other's company. The promise of winter so close at hand held no fear or dread for their young hearts and minds.

David's first love (first after Beryl) was engineering and he had entered his new assignment with unusual enthusiasm. His big opportunity, be felt, was at Hastings—the town that lay just ahead of them over the break of the hill. David had all of his plans perfectly outlined in his mind and he was certain they would work out just that way. He discussed the last minute details with Beryl as they came into Hastings.

"There's Bradley Real Estate Office. Let's stop there," David said, "we'll have a house in short order and we'll have time to look it over and maybe pick out some furniture today."

"Optimistic soul!" murmured Beryl.

Mr. Bradley smiled kindly as he offered them chairs in his office. "I'm David Mason. This is my wife, Beryl. We want to rent a house", David explained before he was seated.

"Houses to rent are practically non-existent in Hastings. We have a few to sell—nice properties at average prices". Mr. Bradley informed them.

David couldn't keep the disappointment from his voice as he exclaimed, "No houses to rent? Surely the housing shortage couldn't have reached this far West!"

"It has, apparently. Families are doubling up—people are clamoring for places to live. Can't offer you a thing unless you want to buy." Mr. Bradley shook his head.

"No, thank you", David muttered, "We'll have to rent."

"Sorry, Mr. Mason. I'll keep you in mind and if I find anything, I'll let you know."

Beryl shared David's disappointment but they both firmly believed that surely something would turn up and they were still hopeful as they started driving on through town.

"Let's look the town over, Beryl. We will be here a week and we may as well find a place to hang our hats for a few days." David smiled at Beryl with the light of love in his eyes.

After a few blocks, the street blended into a Y. David looked questioningly at Beryl, and without a word, she shrugged and pointed to the left. Their course lead them to the outskirts of town and as David was about to turn around, Beryl exclaimed,

"Oh, David, look at the white house on the knoll. It seems empty—let's take a look at it."

"We may get our ears shot off but we'll take a chance," David decided.

The house, not more than 20 years old, was in good condition. The lawn was mowed and the flowers, although faded now, had been well cared for. The house had all the appearances of a lovely home. The shades were drawn almost to the bottom of the windows but David could see the house was nicely furnished with a wholesome 'lived-in' air. The dust covering the furniture somehow couldn't lessen the atmosphere of friendliness that clung to the place.

"Perfect", murmured Beryl, "Let's see if we can find out who owns it."

They scrambled hand in hand to the car, laughing as they ran. It was good to be alive—and young—and together again after David's military stretch.

They drove almost a half mile to the nearest neighbor's and David started up the walk. An elderly man sat on the front porch rocking gently, smoking his pipe.

"Good morning. I'm David Mason. I drove past the white house on the knoll and wondered if you could tell me if it's for rent and who owns it."

"Interested in the Dave Pratt house, eh? I'm Chet Weston. Come up an' set."

David seated himself with his hat in his hand.

"So your name's David . . ."

"Yes, Sir—David Mason. Can you tell me who owns the Pratt house? We would like to rent it if possible."

"Jest got outa the service, didn't ye, Son?"

"Yes. About the house . . ."

"Your wife with ye?"

"Yes . . . . the house is vacant, I see. Can it be rented?"

Chet Weston was silent as he rocked gently, smoked his pipe slowly and looked past David into space. After several minutes, a perplexed frown darkened David's brow as he twirled his hat nervously in his hand. The old man finally spoke without moving his eyes or changing his expression.

"Guess th' house could be rented—if yuh want it . . . . I'll tell ye about thet house, Son . . . . Built it for ma' daughter as a weddin' present 15 years ago. Erminnie, her name was—beautiful girl. Married Dave Pratt and went there tuh live. Two happier people yuh never saw—too much in love fur their own good, I said. Five years they lived there—did well, too—never heard 'em quarrel:—most perfect marriage ever made, thet one was.

About this time o' year 'twas, we had a bad storm . . . . the wind blew a hole in th' roof of th' barn . . . . Dave went tuh fix it . . . . 'Minnie came to th' door to call Dave tuh dinner and saw him fall off thet barn roof. She screamed—most blood curdlin' scream yuh ever heard . . . she ran to Dave callin' his name . . . . Heard her way down here and took off across the field on old Nell bareback. As I got t' her, she was holding Dave in her arms sobbin' . . . . pleadin' with him t' speak tuh her . . . when she 'came aware o' me, she lay Dave down slow-like and whispered, "Dad, he's . . . he's dead."

"After Dave's funeral, 'Minnie's baby was born . . . . too soon . . . .' Minnie and her son went to join Dave. 'Tis a comfort t' me to know they'll all be in Heaven as a family ag'in . . . ." The old man's voice broke.

Silence followed as the old man fought to control his emotions. He looked at David a moment then back into space.

"Ever' storm we've had since, yuh kin hear 'Minnie scream thet same awful scream and hear the Church bell toll Dave's funeral . . . ."

David cleared his throat. "I don't believe in visitation from the supernatural", he said kindly, "Do you mind if I stay there tonight?"

"Can iff'n yuh want tuh, Son. Yuh can hear her scream near the barn where Dave fell . . . . yur wife can stay here."

That night after he heard Beryl's even breathing, David eased out of bed, donned his trousers and jacket, picked up his shoes and quietly slipped out of the house. Sitting on the porch steps, he slipped into his shoes and hurried to the car. He let the car roll out of the drive and started toward the Pratt house. He recognized the barn, a long two-story frame building. He played his flashlight over the outside and decided to enter. An inspection of the interior disclosed nothing of particular interest,

Dave Pratt's tools hung where he had left them, nothing seemed changed. David climbed the steps to the second story and finding no clue, decided to sit down and wait to see if perhaps he might get an introduction to Erminnie. His eyelids drooped and after a few minutes, he fell asleep.

A piercing scream and a cry, "DAVID" woke him with a start. He jumped to his feet to get his bearings and whispered hoarsely, "I still don't believe it!"

He bolted down the stairs and as he jumped the last five steps, he caught the glimpse of a woman dressed in white and for several seconds, did not recognize the figure to be Beryl. She sat on the floor with her arms around her knees. As he reached her, she exclaimed, "David, whatever are you doing in this awful place at this hour of the morning!?!"

"A good question well put, fair Lady, but I should ask you the same question."

"I missed you, David, and went downstairs to find you. Mr. Weston told me you had come here. I tripped over this . . . . this . . . . pile of . . . ."

"Hay rope", David corrected.

"Hay rope . . ." Beryl continued, "and I guess I sprained my ankle. Now just what are you doing here???"

David picked Beryl up and as they drove back to the Westons, he explained his theory. "Most eerie experiences have a logical explanation." he told her.

"David", Beryl scolded, "You know I like to hunt ghosts, too! I'll go back with you tomorrow night."

The next night the Masons were both upstairs in the barn. In spite of Beryl's heavy wraps, her teeth chattered too much to talk to David so she was content to hold his hand.

"There's a storm brewing. We may meet Erminnie tonight." David said softly.

"Uh huh."

"Almost midnight."

"Uh huh."

"Cold?"

"Uh huh." David put his arms around Beryl and drew her closer.

The rain began to fall in torrents and the wind whistled menacingly. They could feel Erminnie's chilly presence. The wind took on increased velocity, and almost in their eardrums, they heard Erminnie scream—once—twice. Beryl grasped David's hand in her icy fingers. The bell began to toll softly at first, louder as the storm increased.

"Stay here. I want to find that bell." David had to shout above the wind.

"Oh, no! I'll go with you. I don't like Erminnie's company." Beryl shouted back.

They lighted their way down the stairs and were guided to the far end of the lower floor by the sound of the bell. David flashed his light in the direction of the sound and saw Dave Pratt's scythe hanging on a nail near a broken window. The current created by the strong wind swung the scythe in rhythm and as the blade struck the beam, the result was very much like the ringing of a bell.

As David reached for the scythe, the shock of another piercing scream ran through him. He grasped the scythe firmly in his hands and let it slide to the floor.

"Now to find Erminnie", David said as they started toward the steps. Upstairs again, the wind seemed to have lessened and David couldn't determine the source of the scream. But as the wind started to blow harder, again Erminnie screamed. David caught the window in the beam of his light and saw a brown object finding its way carefully across the window pane—as Erminnie screamed again. David raised the window with some effort and was almost knocked off his feet as the brown object swung at him.

"There's our ghost", David explained to Beryl, "a sharp tree branch scraping the window pane in the wind, the banging of a scythe against a beam and a lot of small-town imagination. Erminnie moves out tonight—we move in tomorrow."

Beryl chuckled. "And tack a sign on the door 'The Great Mason Detective Agency".

++++

Chapter 8

The Christopher Family

Between the ages of seven and nine, my Father had to have his leg amputated three times. That experience inspired me to write Pioneer Courage.

Pioneer Courage

Rev. Christopher and his family began their nightly prayer meeting at 7:30 as was their custom. The Minister stood behind the hand-made Bible stand as he read the passage of Scripture. His wife, Lucinda, sat near his right at the melodeon. The three children, Anna, 11, William, 7, and Ernest, 5, sat in a semi-circle facing their Father.

The duet by the Minister and his wife that always followed the Scripture reading although simple and direct, was heart-stirring. Lucinda's alto voice blended very well with her husband's and the inspiration they felt as they sang, filled the room. The sweet smile that crossed Lucinda's face as she finished the hymn and looked up at her husband had become a vital part of the evening ritual.

Rev. Christopher's deep musical voice, "Shall we pray?" brought the children to their knees in front of their chairs with their elbows resting on the seats. They closed their eyes and listened as thanks were offered for the little everyday things and the bigger blessings as well. God's blessing and guidance was asked for the entire family, each in turn.

Ernest's five-year old mind never ceased to wonder why his Father always made such a long prayer and invariably at this point, he would begin to wonder if he shouldn't have a serious talk with his Father about the length of his prayers.

While he was debating the subject, he traced his name with his fingernail on the seat of his chair. He could spell his Father's name, his sister's, and his brother's, but he decided against trying his Mother's—too many difficult letters to remember.

The floor seemed hard under William's knees and he shifted his weight. His hands, although in perfect praying order a few minutes ago, were now crossed over his face with the fingers spread—affording excellent observation of Ernest's doodling.

Hardly had the deep "A-men" been uttered before William turned to his Father with, "Ernest wasn't paying attention half the time, Father."

"How do you know that, Son?" The sharp reproachful look in his Father's eyes made William's answer seem to come from afar . . .

"I was watching him."

*   *   *

The afternoon sun shone down brightly on two small boys at play. They were building a Church just as their Father had done. Ernest, the self-appointed roofer, accidentally knocked the entire building down and there followed a quick heated argument. Like most arguments of its kind, it was short and direct.

"You did that on purpose!"

"I did not!"

"You did too!!!"

"I did NOT'"

'YOU DID TOO!!!!"

The presence of the Minister interrupted the boys and both were silent, looking up at their Father with an expression of mixed guilt and innocence. The Minister knelt between the two boys, taking them both in his arms.

"You know it's wrong to quarrel, don't you? If you have any further trouble, bring it to me. I'm sure we can settle it in a much more satisfactory manner than this."

The boys agreed whereupon they were left to continue their play. Things went along smoothly until the building, for the second time, was almost ready for the roof. They became aware they were being watched and the discovery that it was the neighborhood bully, Tommy, disturbed neither of the boys a great deal. Remembering their Father's teaching, they invited him to join them.

After a few minutes, Ernest, again plying his roofer's trade, knocked the building down. Tommy pushed Ernest to the ground with a snarl, "Aw, what did you have to do that for?!"

Both boys were on their feet and tackled their aggressor almost simultaneously. Ernest with both arms around Tommy's waist and William with one arm around his neck and one hand in his hair. The progress toward the house was slow and loud and Rev. Christopher came on the run.

"Here, here, what is the meaning of this?'

Because William was the quick thinker, he was the one to answer his Father in these situations.

"Tommy pushed Ernest down because he knocked the roof off the Church again. You said we should bring our trouble to you, and we were trying to, but Tommy wouldn't come. We were only trying to make him come in."

The Minister smiled and said kindly, "Yes, I said bring your trouble to me but I meant it figuratively, not literally", and spent the next several minutes explaining to his sons the meaning of the two big words.

++++

School was not unpleasant for any of the children in spite of the fact that their Mother was the School Teacher and their home afforded the only school house. But the boys were never really sorry when their classes were dismissed and they were allowed a few minutes to play. All the pupils gathered outside the house and decided upon an inspection of the new Church and shed Rev. Christopher and his parish were building.

The Church was not much more than a large log house, standing on a level spot the men of the parish had wrestled from the forest. The shed in the rear, affording protection for the horses against the weather, stood on a level with the Church, the back wall resting in a bank. The roof of the shed was slanting— higher in front, sloping toward the back. The edge of the roof was only about two feet from the ground on the west side, about seven feet on the east side. The children were delighted they could step from the ground to the roof of the building, scramble over the roof and jump to the ground on the other side . . .

They took their turn at jumping and all went well until William took his turn. He tried to out-jump the others, paying no attention to the condition of his landing place. As he jumped to the ground, his foot struck a jagged rock. He lay there startled and hurt. Ernest, following in close pursuit jumped onto him. William's cry of pain made the children realize something was wrong. Some of them gathered around to help while others ran to the house to tell William's parents—who by this time, having heard the commotion, were on their way to investigate.

Rev. Christopher carried William to the house, whispering words of endearment and encouragement because he knew the boy had been badly hurt. The best doctor available was summoned and the boy had the best of care, but in spite of this, a high fever developed and in a short time, it was evident the boy was in serious trouble. A consultation was held. Seven doctors judged the only means of saving the boy's life was an amputation above the ankle. The operation was performed and although the boy rallied nicely, his condition remained only fair. Before a year had passed, the bone infection had spread and it was necessary to amputate again, this time just below the knee. Still the infection spread.

For the third time in a period of two years, Rev. Christopher and his wife sat by their son's bedside facing the realization that tomorrow meant another amputation. The chances of saving the boy's life were slim. The doctors in the next room were debating whether to disjoint the leg at the hip. When Rev. Christopher was given the full explanation, he said, "No! Leave him enough stump to wear an artificial leg . . . if he lives.

The Minister and his wife could hear the murmur of the voices in the next room as they watched the boy's feverish restlessness. It seemed unjust for a youngster that was 'all boy' to be maimed for life.

For a moment as the Father's mind wandered back through the boy's short life, a smile crossed his face as he remembered the deviltry William and Ernest had been into—the time when they had found a large adder and the boys had armed themselves with long switches. William struck the snake and ran. As the snake chased and nearly reached him, Ernest whacked the snake on the tail and ran, squealing, in the opposite direction. Then William whacked the snake just before it reached Ernest and ran. The boys had a path worn in the hard, brown earth and nearly exhausted the snake when Rev. Christopher found them.

And the Sunday morning the boys had played sick instead of going to Church—they were having such a hilarious time teasing the family goat they didn't notice their Father had returned and stood watching them. One of the boys stood on the edge of the steep bank of the creek, bent over with his hands between his legs and flapped his hands to draw the goat's attention. The goat would look, paw the ground, lower his head and charge. Just before the goat reached him, the boy jumped sidewise and the goat landed in the creek. The stream, being narrow and deep, carried the goat some distance down stream before he could scramble up the bank. No more had he got up on the bank and started away when one of the boys again bent over and flapped his hands. The goat, having an exceptionally short memory and hot temper, would look, then charge, and again go into the water.

When the Minister thought it time to stop this foolishness, he scolded the boys and sent them to the house with the promise of punishment later. He watched the boys disappear and looked at the goat, where it stood, soaking wet, still snorting, near the shed. The more he thought about it, the more the situation amused him. He smiled as he looked toward the house to make sure no one was watching.

He walked to the edge of the bank, bent over and flapped his swallow-tail coat tails. The goat looked, and then CHARGED. The Minister, laughing, looking through his knees at the oncoming goat, neglected to jump sidewise and went over the bank, arms and legs flaying the air—plop—into the water.—splashing and sputtering—to the point of exit.

He went to the house, thoroughly soaked and entirely chagrined. The topic of punishment never came up.

Yes, William had been a lively, active boy but a good one after all. He had shown unusual patience for a youngster in his illness and although bedridden the greater part of the time since his fall two years ago, had kept up with his studies and was even with the other pupils in his class.

After the first amputation, William had said, "Father, I'm going to be a doctor when I grow up—a good one too, and maybe I can save someone from the trouble I'm having." 'How much like him', Rev. Christopher thought 'always thinking of someone else, little mindful of his own feelings.'

As the small, frail hand moved down to touch the leg that wasn't there, the Minister's heart broke anew and he bowed his head to pray, in silence, a most earnest prayer. Then he felt relieved in body and quieted in spirit as he watched his son. The restlessness subsided slightly and the boy's eyelids fluttered open.

"Dad . . ."

"Yes, Son?"

"Don't be afraid, Dad . . ."

Rev. Christopher couldn't speak for several moments as he struggled with the lump in his throat. Lucinda came near her husband and laid her hand on his shoulder. Both were silent for several minutes. Lucinda spoke to her husband softly, "Will we ever find the courage to go through this again?"

William smiled a rather weak, but encouraging smile and answered his Mother's question with, "No, we won't FIND the courage, Mother, we won't have to—because we've never lost it!"

Chapter 9

Later—The Move East

Just when or why the Christopher and Pine families moved to New York State, I never did hear. I do know that Rev. Pine preached for many years in the Presbyterian Church in Union Center, New York. He, his family and several of the cousins are buried in the cemetery near the Church.

Granddad Christopher founded and preached for years in the Presbyterian Church on the corner of Liberty Ave. and Main Street in Union, New York. After Daddy Bennett passed away, Mother Bennett and I moved to an apartment across the street and I started attending Granddad's Church. He had long ago left us for higher ground, unfortunately.

The members of any importance had their own pew with their name on the swinging door. Uncle Ernest lived on Liberty Ave., across the street from the Church and being not only a prominent doctor, a pillar in the community, and the son, no less, of the founder, he had his own pew. The first time I attended Church, I went down the aisle until I found the Christopher name, opened the door and sat down. I felt SO important! . . . Me, sitting in a Church pew with my name on the door! Two ushers standing at another front entrance were watching me. They looked at each other, then both came to the end of the pew. Two grown men needed to evict a seven year old child?

One of them asked my name. I proudly answered, "Christopher. I'm Marian Christopher, niece of Dr. Ernest Christopher." Was it wrong of me to feel smug and smile a little as the 'bouncers' retreated to their station by the door?

++++

Odds and Ends

I can't leave you without one more incident—when I made a 50 year old man blush. On one of the few occasions when I was between jobs, I applied for one that sounded worth investigating. The man seemed very interested in me at the time of the interview, but after not hearing from him for several days, I went to inquire about it. I was ushered into his office at once and when I asked if he had made a decision, he said, "Yes, I found someone with more experience."

'Not likely, but possible', I thought. As 1 was gathering myself to leave, the side door opened and in walked this scantily dressed young thing not over 17 or 18 and it was obvious from his reaction that she was his secretary.

More experience? I was working in industry before she was born! At this point, he evidently realized he had been caught because he sucked in his breath and looked at me. Did I notice the inference? Of course I did. I may be ignorant but I'm not stupid.

I skewered him to his seat with one of my special looks. Then, my eyes were such a dark blue they looked black. Believe me, I gave him a black look. His face turned a bright red. Saying not a word, I got up and left him to live with his lie.

++++

Well, maybe just one more incident won't hurt, after all the Dionne Quintuplets were history. We had been following their progress since their birth. One day, after I came home from work, Mother Bennett suggested we go see them. I must have had the idea that the children were housed just over the border because we started out not realizing how far we had to go or what the cost would be. (I realize now, I really kept my guardian Angel busy in my younger days.)

We traveled into Canada with no problem, but from there we traveled and traveled, going from paved highways to hardly more than a cow path when we broke over a knoll, into a small settlement where the children were housed. The hospital was a large, one story building with a large circular glass-enclosed room in front.

There was quite a crowd standing outside and the guard told us the girls couldn't see us. That wasn't true, because one girl held her book up to the window and when their nurse appeared in the driveway, they started singing her a song, in French, of course.

At that time, I had a Chevy coupe with a rumble seat. A light car with extremely good gas mileage, thankfully. It was equipped with an air horn that sounded like a Mac truck. We started home over the bumpy country roads. For several miles, every time I hit a bump, the horn blew. Since I'm just the nut that holds the wheel, I didn't know what to do except keep driving. We finally dropped into a small gathering of houses and the horn took off with a vengeance. Heads popped out of every window in that settlement. Finally, I pulled over in front of one of the houses and the man of the house came out and immediately came to my rescue. He asked me to pop the hood. He knew just what to do and pulled the horn wire loose.

Seeing we were from the States, he started to chat. While we were talking, he noticed his horse was rubbing his rump against the fence in the pasture at least half a football field away. It would have taken very little more pressure to knock the fence down. He picked up a stone and threw it left-handed and hit the horse on the rump. The action didn't interrupt his conversation one bit. While we were talking, the wife came out of the house. She was taller than her husband. When she noticed how tall I was, she asked if all Americans were tall. I assured her that we had all sizes and shapes in America. She sidled up to me. Looking up at me with a wry smile, she said, "I like to stand next to you, you make me feel so normal."

Since it was getting on toward evening, we decided we better stay over and drive home in the day light. We found a cabin and rented it for the night. It was equipped with a coffee pot, lights and hot water. We were looking forward to a hot cup of coffee before we started home. The bed was comfortable and we both had a good night's sleep. But just as day was breaking, the management turned off the electricity, so we were denied our hot coffee.

Starting for home, I noticed the gas gauge was telling me we needed fuel and before long, we found a station. The price of gas was higher in Canada than in America and I argued a little with the attendant but decided I had no choice but to buy five gallons. Since Canadian gallons contain five quarts, unlike America's four, we made it home with no trouble.

Chapter 10

My Most Significant Experience

I really can't close without relating the most significant experience of my life. Weird but true. The summer I turned 17, we had moved to a farm in Glen Aubrey, New York. One Sunday afternoon, I was out on the front lawn when a car with two young men pulled up. They invited me to the special meetings they were starting the next week in the little Church about a mile up the road. Having nothing better to do, I promised to go.

These two young men from Practical Bible School in Johnson City, New York, had been out for a joy ride one afternoon and had seen this little Church all boarded up ready for sale. They got down on their knees on the Church steps and covenanted with the Lord, if He would open the way for them to come back after graduation, they would hold special meetings there.

Of course, the Lord honors a request like that and the young men came with mops, pails and all sorts of cleaning supplies and blitzed up the Church. They even varnished the pews but they used the wrong varnish. They should have used shellac. The warm June weather molded the warm bodies to the pews and when the people stood for the hymns, it was rip, rip, rip all over the place.

I walked to the Church the first night of the meetings, and sat down in one end of one of the pews. During the service, I became convicted. Oh, I believed in God and I knew Christ died for the whole world, but it was that night, for the first time I realized that Christ died for ME. It was a personal thing and had to be settled personally.

I promised myself that before they finished the invitation hymn, I would go forward. The congregation started the chorus but my feet felt glued to the floor. I began to think,

"I know I should go forward, but if I do, the Preacher will make me stay after the meeting and I didn't do the dishes before I left."

The Preacher said, "Maybe you're thinking about the work you have to do, never mind the Lord will take care of that." Then I thought,

"What will I do for entertainment?" The Preacher said, "Maybe you're wondering what you will do for entertainment, never mind the Lord will take care of that." Next I thought, "But what will my friends think?" The Preacher said, "Maybe you're thinking about what your friends will say. Never mind, the Lord will take care of that"

"But how can I tell my Mother?" I thought. The Preacher said, "Maybe you're thinking about what your parents will say, never mind the Lord will take care of that." Every argument the devil put in my mind, the Preacher answered from the pulpit.

By this time, the hymn was nearly finished. Out of the corner of my eye, I saw this big man step next to me. He gave me a push out into the aisle. I turned around to give him an elbow jab in the midsection he wouldn't soon forget—but there wasn't another person in my entire half of the pew. I could see the space the man had occupied slowly disappear.

Here I am, out in the aisle, hanging onto the back of the pew ahead of me. Then I heard a sweet voice say, "You have come this far, why not go all the way." And I did. The Church probably wouldn't seat more than 50 people at full capacity, so the aisles weren't very long, but before I reached the front, I knew I was saved! I felt the Holy Spirit enter my body as the Scripture's promise.

The Preacher didn't keep me very long and I walked home. I really don't remember my feet touching the ground that entire mile. As I looked around, the grass seemed so much greener, the sky so much bluer, the wild flowers so much prettier, even the black and white cows looked blacker and whiter than I had remembered.

When I walked in the kitchen, I hadn't taken 6 steps before I told my Mother, "I accepted Christ tonight." She was pleased as she, too, was a Christian.

I'm sure I've disappointed my Lord many times during my lifetime but He has never disappointed me.

Th . . . th . . . th . . . that's all folks.

++++

I trust all my readers will get a blessing out of My Memoirs which I thoroughly enjoyed writing, and glean a glimpse of the rich heritage that is ours from our ancestors.

—Marian C. Pilcher

Made in the USA
Lexington, KY
20 July 2013